Don't Give It Away

What Every Independent Artist Must Know About Contracts, Copyright, and Creative Control

BY NICHOLAS SALERNO III

DON'T GIVE IT AWAY

First edition. March 3, 2026.

ISBN: 979-8233214509

Written by Nicholas Salerno III.

Table of Contents

Dedicated to all my creative friends and family — and to **Jason Story**, for helping musicians find their voice and protect their work.

Introduction
I Learned This the Hard Way

I've written books.

I've built businesses.

I've painted houses.

I've drafted contracts.

I've mediated disputes.

I've created stories, music, characters, worlds, and ideas that didn't exist before I sat down and made them real.

And here's what I wish someone told me early:

Creative talent is not enough.

If you don't understand your rights, someone else will.

I didn't grow up thinking about intellectual property. I was focused on building — building projects, building stories, building momentum. When you're hungry and ambitious, you say yes to opportunity. You say yes to exposure. You say yes to "standard contracts." You say yes to people who sound confident.

And sometimes, that yes quietly transfers everything you just created.

Not because you're stupid.

Because you're excited.

I've seen it from both sides now.

I've seen creatives lose control of their work because they didn't understand what they signed.

I've seen businesses assume they owned something simply because they paid for it.

I've mediated disputes where both sides felt right — and both sides misunderstood the contract.

And I've realized something important:

Most creative conflicts aren't about bad people.

They're about unclear agreements.

This book isn't written from an ivory tower. It's written from experience — from building brands, launching projects, negotiating deals, writing contracts, resolving disputes, and watching how ownership decisions ripple forward years later.

Whether you're:

- An independent musician
- A writer
- A designer
- A filmmaker
- A podcaster
- A digital creator
- Or just getting started

You are not "just" creating content.

You are creating property.

Property has value.

Property needs structure.

Property needs protection.

When I started creating, I thought the hard part was making something good.

That's only half the game.

The other half is keeping control of what you make.

I've written about addiction, conflict resolution, construction disputes, business structure, legal frameworks — and across all of it, one theme keeps showing up:

Clarity creates power.

This book is clarity for creatives.

Not legal jargon.

Not fear-based paranoia.

Not complicated theory.

Just practical understanding:

- What you own
- What you give away
- What to watch for
- How to structure deals
- How to respond when something goes wrong
- And how to build long-term creative freedom

You don't need to become a lawyer.

You need to become informed.

The moment you understand ownership, licensing, work-for-hire, and contract red flags — you move differently.

You negotiate differently.

You sign differently.

You enforce differently.

You build differently.

I wish I had this framework when I started.

Not because I failed — but because I could have built even stronger, faster, and with more leverage.

Now you have it.

Let's protect what you create.

Let's build it the right way.

Let's go.

Chapter 1

You Own It (Usually)

Most creative people don't realize this:

The moment you create something original and fix it in tangible form — you own it.

You don't need to file paperwork.

You don't need to mail it to yourself.

You don't need a lawyer.

If you wrote it, recorded it, designed it, illustrated it, filmed it, composed it, coded it, or photographed it — and it exists in a tangible form — you automatically own the copyright.

That's powerful.

But most creatives act like they don't.

What Copyright Actually Protects

Copyright protects original works of authorship fixed in a tangible medium.

That includes:

- Songs and sound recordings
- Lyrics and written works
- Paintings and illustrations
- Graphic design
- Logos (sometimes overlapping with trademark law)
- Films and video
- Podcasts
- Software code
- Photography

If it's original and fixed in some way (written, recorded, saved, uploaded), it's protected.

You own:

- The right to reproduce it
- The right to distribute it
- The right to display it
- The right to perform it
- The right to create derivative works

That bundle of rights is your leverage.

What You Don't Automatically Own

You don't own:

- Ideas
- Concepts
- Titles
- General styles
- Methods

You own the expression — not the idea.

You can't own "a song about heartbreak."

You can own your specific lyrics and melody.

That distinction matters.

Ownership vs. Registration

This is where people get confused.

You own your work the moment you create it.

Registration is different.

Registration gives you:

- Stronger enforcement rights
- The ability to file a lawsuit

- Potential statutory damages
- A public record of ownership

Ownership exists automatically.

Registration strengthens your position.

Think of it this way:

Creation = Ownership.

Registration = Armor.

The Creative Mistake

Most artists create something and then immediately say:

"Yeah, they can use it."

That phrase is dangerous.

Because "use it" can mean:

- For one campaign
- Forever
- Worldwide
- With modifications
- With sublicensing rights

Or something completely different.

When you casually grant permission, you're potentially granting rights without defining scope.

That's where creators lose control.

The Emotional Trap

Here's the real reason creatives give away rights:

Excitement.

A label is interested.

A brand calls.

A client wants your design.

A producer says, "We love your sound."

And your brain goes:
"I don't want to mess this up."
So you say yes before you understand what you're giving away.
Ownership isn't about ego.
It's about control over:

- Future income
- Future licensing
- Portfolio rights
- Creative direction
- Long-term leverage

The Independent Contractor Reality

If you are a freelancer — musician, designer, writer, videographer — and you are not a W-2 employee working within the scope of employment, you generally own your work unless you sign something transferring it.

That "something" is usually:

- A work-for-hire clause
- A copyright assignment
- A broad IP transfer clause

If you didn't sign one, ownership likely remains with you.
That's important.
Because many companies assume they own what they paid for.
Payment does not equal ownership.
Payment buys what the contract says it buys.

Practical Shift in Thinking

Stop thinking:
"I got paid, so they own it."
Start thinking:

"I got paid for what exactly?"

Was it:

- A limited license?
- A one-time use?
- A perpetual right?
- A full assignment?

If it's not written clearly, it's ambiguous.

Ambiguity creates disputes.

Clarity protects you.

A Simple Rule

Before delivering final files, ask:

"What rights am I granting?"

If you can't answer that in one sentence, you need clarity.

For example:

"I'm granting a non-exclusive license for online use for one year."

That's clear.

Compare that to:

"Yeah, you can use it."

Not clear.

Why This Matters Long-Term

Imagine you design a logo for $800.

Five years later, the company scales, raises capital, and builds a national brand around your logo.

If you assigned ownership permanently for $800, you are done.

If you licensed it properly, you may have leverage for renegotiation.

Ownership determines future opportunity.

Chapter 1 Takeaway

You are not "just an artist."

You are a creator of intellectual property.

The moment you create something original and fix it in tangible form, you own it.

Your job now is to protect it.

Chapter 2

The Trap: Work-for-Hire

There are two words that quietly strip creators of ownership more than almost anything else:

Work for hire.

They look harmless.

Professional.

Standard.

Routine.

They are not.

If you sign a proper work-for-hire agreement, you are not the legal author of your own work.

Read that again.

You created it — but legally, someone else is considered the author from the beginning.

What Work-for-Hire Actually Means

Under U.S. law, work-for-hire applies in only two situations:

1. You Are an Employee

If you're a W-2 employee acting within the scope of your job, your employer owns what you create for that job.

That's straightforward.

2. You Are an Independent Contractor — AND

There is:

- A written agreement

- Explicitly stating the work is "work made for hire"
- AND the work fits within specific statutory categories

Here's the part people miss:

Independent contractor work is NOT automatically work-for-hire.

It must meet legal requirements.

And it must be in writing.

If there is no written clause saying "work made for hire," ownership typically stays with the creator.

Why Companies Use It

Because it gives them:

- Full ownership
- No royalty obligations
- No renegotiation later
- No future leverage from you
- Complete control forever

For businesses, it's clean.

For creatives, it can be permanent surrender.

The Dangerous Language

Watch for phrases like:

- "Work made for hire."
- "Contractor hereby assigns all right, title, and interest."
- "All rights worldwide in perpetuity."
- "Including all renewals and extensions thereof."

"In perpetuity" means forever.

Not five years.

Not ten.

Forever.

The Emotional Setup

Here's how it usually happens.

A client says:

"We just need a standard contract."

You glance at it.

It looks formal.

It feels official.

You don't want to appear difficult.

So you sign.

What you may have just done:

Transferred full ownership of your music, design, script, logo, or artwork permanently — for a one-time fee.

No royalties.

No backend.

No renegotiation.

No leverage.

Payment Does Not Equal Fair Value

If someone wants full ownership, that is a premium transaction.

Full assignment should cost significantly more than limited use.

Think of it like selling a house versus renting it.

If you sell the house, you no longer benefit from appreciation.

If you rent it, you retain ownership and future income potential.

Work-for-hire is selling the house.

Most creatives sell the house for the price of a month's rent.

The Hidden Combo Clause

Sometimes companies use both:

1. "This is a work made for hire."
2. "If not considered work for hire, contractor assigns all rights."

That second sentence is a backup trap.

Even if the work doesn't legally qualify as work-for-hire, the assignment clause transfers ownership anyway.

If you see both together, ownership is being fully transferred.

When Work-for-Hire Makes Sense

There are situations where it's reasonable:

- You are hired as part of a production team.
- You are paid premium rates.
- You have no desire to retain rights.
- It's a clear transactional exchange.

The key is not avoiding work-for-hire.

The key is understanding what you are trading.

What You Can Do Instead

Instead of full work-for-hire, consider:

- Limited license agreements
- Exclusive licenses for defined time periods
- Territory restrictions
- Usage-based pricing
- Royalty participation
- Reversion clauses

You can say:
"I'm happy to grant a license, but I retain ownership."
That changes everything.

Red Flag Scenario

If someone pushes hard for:

- Immediate signature
- No negotiation
- Broad rights language
- No discussion of scope

Pause.
Control over your intellectual property is not something to rush.

The Mindset Shift

You are not being difficult when you protect your work.
You are being professional.
Serious businesses negotiate rights all the time.
Only uninformed creatives sign blindly.

Chapter 2 Takeaway

Work-for-hire is not evil.
But it is powerful.
If you sign it, you are giving up ownership.
Before you do, ask yourself:
Am I being compensated at a level that reflects permanent transfer?
If the answer is no, renegotiate.

Chapter 3
Ownership vs. Licensing

There is one fundamental difference that determines whether you stay in control of your career or slowly give it away:

Ownership transfers control.

Licensing preserves it.

If you understand this chapter deeply, you will negotiate differently forever.

Ownership (Assignment)

Ownership means you no longer control the intellectual property.

When you assign ownership:

- You give up your copyright.
- The other party becomes the legal owner.
- They can use it however they want.
- They can modify it.
- They can sell it.
- They can sublicense it.
- They can stop using it.
- They can lock you out of it.

And you typically receive a one-time payment.

That's it.

No future leverage.

No backend participation.

No upside if the project explodes.

You sold the house.

Licensing

Licensing means:

You keep ownership.

You grant permission to use the work.

That permission can be:

- Limited
- Specific
- Conditional
- Time-bound
- Territory-based
- Usage-restricted

Licensing keeps you in the game.

The Four Questions Every Creative Must Ask

Before granting rights, clarify:

1. **Scope** – What exactly are they allowed to do?
2. **Duration** – For how long?
3. **Territory** – Where?
4. **Exclusivity** – Are you allowed to license it to others?

If you can't answer those four questions clearly, you're granting too much.

Exclusive vs. Non-Exclusive

This matters more than most creatives realize.

Non-Exclusive License

You can license the same work to multiple parties.

You retain flexibility.

You maintain market value.

Exclusive License

Only that party can use it in the defined scope.

You cannot license it elsewhere within that scope.

Exclusive licenses are more valuable.

Charge accordingly.

Perpetual vs. Term-Based

Perpetual = Forever.

Term-Based = Defined period.

If someone wants perpetual exclusive rights, they are asking for near-ownership.

Price it accordingly.

Or don't agree to it.

Territory

Global rights are worth more than local rights.

If someone only needs North American rights, don't automatically grant worldwide rights.

Be specific.

Derivative Works

This is where creators get surprised.

If you allow derivative works, you're allowing:

- Remixes
- Modifications
- Adaptations
- Rebranding
- Sequels
- Spin-offs

Sometimes that's fine.

Sometimes it's not.

Define it.

Portfolio Rights

Never forget this.

Even if you transfer ownership, negotiate the right to:

- Display the work in your portfolio
- Use it for self-promotion
- Reference it in marketing

Otherwise, you may legally be unable to show your own work.

Yes, that happens.

A Simple Pricing Philosophy

If you assign ownership:

Charge premium.

If you grant exclusive perpetual license:

Charge near premium.

If you grant limited license:

Charge based on scope and duration.

Don't price a Ferrari like a rental car.

The Silent Danger: "All Media Now Known or Hereafter Devised"

That phrase appears often in contracts.

It means:

They can use your work in formats that don't even exist yet.

Streaming.

VR.

AI.

Future platforms.

Is that fine? Maybe.

But understand what you're agreeing to.

The Power Move

Instead of saying:

"How much will you pay me?"

Ask:

"What rights are you asking for?"

That shifts the negotiation.

You are not selling time.

You are licensing intellectual property.

Real-World Scenario

You design a logo.

Client says:

"We just need it for our website."

That's limited digital usage.

But if the contract says:

"All rights in all media worldwide in perpetuity."

That includes:

- Merchandise
- Packaging
- Franchising
- Licensing
- Resale
- Corporate expansion

Those are not the same transaction.

The Long Game

Licensing builds recurring opportunity.

Ownership transfer ends it.

Many independent creators don't build wealth because they transfer ownership early for small money.

Ownership creates leverage.

Leverage creates negotiating power.

Negotiating power creates long-term income.

Chapter 3 Takeaway

If you remember one thing:

Ownership is final.

Licensing is strategic.

You don't need to be aggressive.

You need to be informed.

Chapter 4
Contract Red Flags

Contracts are not scary.

Blind signing is.

Most creative contracts aren't evil. They're written to protect the party who drafted them.

If that wasn't you, assume the language leans in their favor.

Your job isn't to panic.

Your job is to recognize red flags.

◈ Red Flag #1: "All Rights Worldwide in Perpetuity"

This phrase means:

- Everywhere
- Forever
- In every format
- With no expiration

That is not a small clause.

That is permanent transfer.

If the payment is small and the rights are unlimited, something is misaligned.

◈ Red Flag #2: "Work Made for Hire" + Assignment Backup

If you see:

"This work shall be considered work made for hire. If not deemed work for hire, contractor assigns all rights..."

That is full ownership transfer no matter what.

No confusion.
No gray area.
If you sign that, you are done.
Ask yourself:
Am I being paid appropriately for permanent surrender?

◈ Red Flag #3: Indemnification Clauses

Indemnification means:
If something goes wrong, you pay.
Some contracts require you to:

- Cover legal fees
- Defend lawsuits
- Pay damages
- Protect the company from claims

Even if you were paid $1,500.
This is dangerous if it's broad and unlimited.
A reasonable clause limits your liability to:

- What you were paid
- Direct damages
- Your own intentional misconduct

Unlimited indemnity can financially destroy a freelancer.

◈ Red Flag #4: Moral Rights Waiver

This means you waive:

- Attribution rights
- Integrity rights
- The right to object to modifications

In plain terms:

They can alter your work, remove your name, distort it — and you have no say.

Sometimes that's acceptable.

Sometimes it's unacceptable.

But you should never waive it casually.

⟐ Red Flag #5: Scope Creep Without Compensation

Look for vague language like:

"Creator agrees to provide revisions as reasonably requested."

How many revisions?

Unlimited?

Reasonable according to whom?

If scope isn't defined, time gets drained.

Define limits.

⟐ Red Flag #6: No Payment Schedule

Contracts that say:

"Payment upon completion."

Completion according to who?

Better structure:

- 50% upfront
- 50% upon delivery
- Clear acceptance timeline

Clarity prevents conflict.

⟐ Red Flag #7: "In All Media Now Known or Hereafter Devised"

We touched on this before.

This extends rights into future technologies.

Streaming wasn't mainstream 25 years ago.

Social media didn't exist.

AI-generated derivatives weren't common.

Do you want to include unknown future media?

Maybe.

But understand it.

⟐ Red Flag #8: No Reversion Clause

If rights are granted exclusively and there is no:

- Time limit
- Performance requirement
- Sales minimum
- Termination right

You may lose control permanently even if the project dies.

Reversion clauses protect you.

⟐ Red Flag #9: Silence About Credit

If the contract doesn't guarantee:

- Attribution
- Name placement
- Portfolio usage

You may legally lose the ability to claim your work.

Always clarify credit rights.

⟐ Red Flag #10: Pressure to Sign Immediately

This isn't in the contract text — it's behavior.

If someone says:

"We need this signed today."

Pause.

Professional deals allow review time.

Urgency often benefits the party pushing it.

The Emotional Test

Before signing, ask:

If this project becomes huge, will I regret these terms?

If the answer is yes, renegotiate.

Negotiation Isn't Confrontation

You can say:

"I'm comfortable granting a license, but not full assignment at this rate."

"I'd like to limit indemnity to the amount paid."

"I'd like to include portfolio rights."

Professional people negotiate.

Only insecure creatives feel guilty doing it.

The 24-Hour Rule

Never sign a contract the same day you receive it.

Even if it's small.

Even if it's friendly.

Even if it's a friend.

Especially if it's a friend.

Chapter 4 Takeaway

Contracts don't steal rights.

Signatures do.

Your power is not in being aggressive.

It's in being informed.

Chapter 5
Protecting Your Work

Protection is not paranoia.

It's professionalism.

Most creatives only think about protection after something goes wrong.

The smarter move?

Build light systems that protect you before conflict ever happens.

You don't need to become a lawyer.

You need structure.

---

1. Put It in Writing — Even If It's Simple

You do not need a 20-page contract for every project.

But you do need clarity.

Even a simple email confirming terms can protect you:

"Just confirming: I'm granting a non-exclusive license for online use for 12 months. Ownership remains with me."

That sentence can prevent a lawsuit.

Written agreements:

- Clarify scope
- Reduce misunderstandings
- Protect relationships
- Protect income

Verbal agreements rely on memory.

Memory fails.

---

2. Define Scope Before You Start

Before you begin work, clarify:

- Who owns it?
- What rights are being granted?
- How long?
- Where?
- Is it exclusive?
- How many revisions?

Scope defined upfront eliminates most disputes later.

---

3. Use Tiered Pricing

If a client wants more rights, charge more.
Example structure:

- Limited digital license – Base rate
- Exclusive 3-year license – Higher rate
- Full ownership transfer – Premium rate

Rights have value.
Price them accordingly.

---

4. Keep Organized Proof of Creation

If ownership is ever challenged, you need evidence.
Keep:

- Draft files
- Time-stamped project files
- Source files
- Metadata
- Email chains
- Project invoices

Cloud backups matter.
Organization is leverage.

---

5. Register When It Matters

You automatically own your work.
But registration strengthens enforcement.
Consider registration when:

- The work has commercial value
- You plan wide distribution
- You anticipate potential disputes
- It's core to your brand

Registration allows access to stronger remedies.
Ownership is automatic.
Enforcement strength is strategic.

---

6. Watermark and Label Drafts

Early drafts should not be:

- Fully unprotected
- High resolution
- Fully transferable

Watermark until final payment clears.
Deliver final files after payment, not before.
This is not distrust.
It's business.

---

7. Invoice Strategically

Your invoice should match your agreement.
Instead of:
"Logo design – $800"
Consider:
"Logo design – Non-exclusive 12-month digital license – $800"
Your invoice can reinforce scope.

---

8. Don't Overshare Source Files

Source files equal power.
If someone wants:

- Editable files
- Raw stems
- Original layered files

That's a bigger rights grant.
Price it that way.

---

9. Use Clear Delivery Language

When delivering work, say:

"Delivery of files does not transfer ownership unless otherwise agreed in writing."

That one sentence changes assumptions.

---

10. Protect Your Portfolio Rights

Always retain the right to:

- Display your work
- Use it in your portfolio
- Promote it on social media
- List it in your resume

Otherwise, you may legally silence yourself.

---

11. Maintain Professional Boundaries

Friends.
Family.
Collaborators.
These are the most common conflict zones.
Put agreements in writing even with people you trust.

Especially with people you trust.

Trust is preserved through clarity.

12. Think Long-Term

Every project is not just a paycheck.

It's an asset.

Ask:

Will I want control of this in five years?

If yes, structure accordingly.

The Shift

Amateurs think:

"How fast can I get paid?"

Professionals think:

"How do I protect future value?"

Protection does not slow you down.

It stabilizes you.

Chapter 5 Takeaway

You don't need complex systems.

You need consistent ones.

Written scope.

Clear rights.

Organized records.

Strategic pricing.

Protection is not about fear.

It's about confidence.

Chapter 6
What If They Use It Without Permission?

It will happen.

Someone will:

- Use your music without paying.
- Repost your art without credit.
- Print your design on merchandise.
- Keep using your logo after the agreement expired.
- Modify your work without permission.
- Claim they "thought they owned it."

Your first reaction will be emotional.

Anger.

Betrayal.

Panic.

Your power is in not reacting emotionally.

Your power is in responding strategically.

Step 1: Confirm the Facts

Before you do anything:

- Review the agreement.
- Check the scope.
- Check the duration.
- Check exclusivity.
- Check whether there was an implied license.

Sometimes it's infringement.

Sometimes it's misunderstanding.

Clarity first.

Reaction second.

Step 2: Preserve Evidence

Take screenshots.

Save URLs.

Document dates.

Download copies.

Archive social posts.

If it disappears later, you still have proof.

Organization equals leverage.

Step 3: Start Professional — Not Aggressive

Do not start with threats.

Start with clarity.

Example:

"I noticed the logo is still being used beyond the agreed 12-month term. I'd like to discuss updating the licensing agreement."

That is calm.

That is controlled.

That signals professionalism.

Step 4: The Cease-and-Desist Letter

If necessary, send a formal notice.

A cease-and-desist letter:

- Identifies your ownership
- Describes unauthorized use
- Demands corrective action
- Sets a deadline

It does not need to be hostile.

It needs to be clear.

Many disputes resolve at this stage.
Because most people are not trying to steal.
They're trying to avoid paying again.

Step 5: Retroactive Licensing

This is powerful.
Instead of saying:
"You owe me damages."
You say:
"Let's resolve this with a retroactive license."
Translation:
Pay now, and we legitimize past use.
This often produces faster resolution than threats.
Businesses prefer settlement to litigation.

Step 6: Mediation Before War

Litigation is expensive.
Slow.
Public.
Emotionally draining.
Mediation is:

- Private
- Faster
- Flexible
- Creative
- Business-oriented

In mediation, you can structure:

- Installment payments
- Expanded licenses
- Future collaboration

- Royalty adjustments
- Public credit corrections

Courts give money or injunctions.
Mediation gives options.

Step 7: When Litigation Makes Sense

Litigation may be necessary if:

- The infringement is massive.
- The infringer refuses to communicate.
- There is significant financial damage.
- The rights are core to your business.
- They are knowingly exploiting your work.

But litigation should be a business decision — not an emotional one.
Ask:
Is this worth the cost, time, and stress?

The Common Mistake

Many creatives jump straight to social media.
They post:
"They stole my work."
That feels powerful.
But it can:

- Complicate negotiations
- Damage credibility
- Create defamation risk
- Reduce settlement flexibility

Keep disputes professional.
Public pressure is rarely strategic long-term.

The Silent Danger: Delay

If someone is using your work without permission and you say nothing for years, your leverage weakens.

Enforce early.

Enforce calmly.

Enforce clearly.

Protecting Your Reputation While Enforcing Your Rights

You can be:

Firm.

Professional.

Calm.

Direct.

You do not need to be dramatic.

Professionals enforce rights without losing composure.

The Power Position

When you understand your rights, enforcement becomes less emotional.

It becomes business.

And business can be negotiated.

Chapter 6 Takeaway

If someone uses your work without permission:

1. Confirm facts.
2. Preserve evidence.
3. Communicate professionally.
4. Offer solutions before threats.
5. Escalate strategically.

Protection is not about aggression.

It's about leverage.

Chapter 7

Smart Strategies for Creative Freedom

Creative freedom is not just artistic.

It's structural.

It's financial.

It's contractual.

Most independent creators don't lose freedom because they lack talent.

They lose it because they give away leverage early.

This chapter is about building leverage intentionally.

---

1. License More. Assign Less.

If you remember one thing from this book:

License whenever possible.

Ownership transfer should be rare and priced high.

Licensing gives you:

- Future income potential
- Renegotiation leverage
- Long-term control
- Portfolio value

If you build a body of work that you still own, you build assets.

Assets create stability.

---

2. Price for Rights — Not Time

Stop thinking hourly.

Start thinking:

"What rights are they buying?"

Example:

If someone wants:

- Exclusive global perpetual rights

That is not a small transaction.

Your pricing should reflect the long-term value of the asset — not the hours spent creating it.

Creative wealth is built on intellectual property, not labor alone.

---

3. Use Time as Leverage

Instead of granting rights forever, try:

- 1-year exclusive license
- 3-year renewal option
- Performance-based extensions
- Automatic reversion if unused

Time limits create negotiation points.

Perpetual grants eliminate them.

---

4. Retain Portfolio and Credit Rights Always

Even if you assign ownership, negotiate:

- Attribution
- Display rights
- Case study rights

Your past work markets your future work.

Never give away your ability to show what you've done.

---

5. Think in Catalogs, Not Projects

Musicians have catalogs.

Writers have catalogs.

Designers have portfolios.

Filmmakers have libraries.

Catalog thinking changes decisions.

You don't ask:

"How much is this worth today?"

You ask:

"What is this worth over 10 years?"

Ownership compounds.

Assignment ends compounding.

6. Separate Creative Control from Business Control

You can negotiate:

- Creative approval rights
- Modification restrictions
- Brand alignment clauses

Sometimes you may license commercial use but retain moral influence.

Not every negotiation is about money.

Some are about integrity.

7. Build Repeat Structures

Instead of reinventing agreements every time, create:

- A standard license template
- A tiered pricing sheet
- A rights menu
- A revision policy

When you have structure, you project professionalism.

Professional creatives attract professional clients.

8. Don't Undervalue Early Work

The "I just need exposure" trap destroys leverage.
Exposure does not pay rent.
Exposure does not equal ownership.
Exposure does not replace licensing value.
If exposure is offered, structure it:

- Limited scope
- Credit guarantees
- Defined usage

Never grant unlimited rights for vague exposure.

9. Diversify Revenue Streams

Creative freedom increases when:

- You license to multiple parties
- You retain rights across projects
- You maintain partial ownership
- You collect royalties
- You build long-term catalogs

The more diversified your rights portfolio, the more resilient your career.

10. Know When to Walk Away

Not every deal is good.
If someone demands:

- Full ownership
- Low payment
- Unlimited indemnity
- No negotiation

That is not opportunity.

That is extraction.

Walking away is power.

The Mindset Shift

You are not just a creator.

You are a rights holder.

You are building intellectual property assets.

You are building leverage.

Creative freedom comes from ownership clarity, licensing strategy, and long-term thinking.

Chapter 7 Takeaway

Freedom is not the absence of contracts.

It is understanding them.

When you control your rights, you control your trajectory.

Chapter 8
The Creative Mindset Shift

I wish I had this book when I got started.

Not because I wasn't talented.

Not because I wasn't working hard.

But because no one explained the business side of creativity in plain language.

No one said:

"You don't lose your rights because you're naive.

You lose them because you're excited."

This final chapter isn't about contracts.

It's about identity.

You're Not "Just" an Artist

You are:

- A creator of intellectual property
- A rights holder
- A negotiator
- A business entity
- A brand

When you create something original and fix it in tangible form, you have created property.

Property deserves protection.

Property deserves strategy.

The Early Mistake

Most creatives think like this at the beginning:

"I just need someone to give me a chance."

So they say yes.

Yes to broad rights.

Yes to low payment.

Yes to permanent ownership transfer.

Yes to "standard contracts."

But here's the truth:

Serious professionals negotiate.

Serious professionals protect rights.

Serious professionals don't sign blindly.

You're not difficult when you ask questions.

You're informed.

Fear vs. Leverage

Fear says:

"If I push back, they'll walk away."

Leverage says:

"If they walk away because I asked reasonable questions, this wasn't the right deal."

The right partners respect clarity.

The wrong partners resist it.

That resistance tells you everything you need to know.

Long-Term Thinking

Every project is not just money.

It's leverage.

It's portfolio.

It's licensing power.

It's catalog building.

It's future negotiation strength.

Think in decades.

Not weeks.

The creatives who build wealth aren't always the most famous.

They're often the ones who retained rights.

Professional Calm

When disputes happen, stay calm.
When contracts arrive, review calmly.
When negotiations start, speak calmly.
Emotion weakens leverage.
Clarity strengthens it.

The Quiet Confidence

When you understand:

- Ownership vs. licensing
- Work-for-hire traps
- Red flags
- Enforcement options
- Strategic structuring

You move differently.
You don't rush.
You don't panic.
You don't overshare.
You don't undersell.
You negotiate from strength.

The New Rule

Before you sign anything, ask:
"What am I giving up?"
If the answer is unclear, pause.
If the answer is "everything," charge accordingly.
If the answer feels unfair, renegotiate.
If they refuse clarity, walk.

You Don't Need to Be Aggressive

You don't need to threaten.

You don't need to posture.
You don't need to be combative.
You need to be informed.
Informed creators are powerful.

Final Thought

Creative freedom isn't just artistic freedom.
It's structural freedom.
It's the ability to:

- Say no.
- License strategically.
- Retain control.
- Build long-term value.
- Protect your work calmly and professionally.

You don't need to know every law.
You need to understand the fundamentals.
And now you do.

Special Features

✔ The Artist Contract Survival Checklist

Before You Sign:

- ☐ Who owns the work?
- ☐ Is this work-for-hire?
- ☐ Is there an assignment clause?
- ☐ What is the scope of use?
- ☐ Is it exclusive or non-exclusive?
- ☐ How long do the rights last?
- ☐ What territories are covered?
- ☐ Is there a reversion clause?
- ☐ Is indemnification limited?
- ☐ Do I retain portfolio rights?
- ☐ Are payment terms clear?
- ☐ Is there a revision limit?

If you cannot answer these clearly — do not sign.

✔ Sample Basic Licensing Language (Plain Example)

"Creator retains ownership of the Work. Client is granted a non-exclusive license to use the Work for digital marketing purposes within North America for a period of 12 months."

✔ Sample Assignment Language (Know What It Looks Like)

"Creator hereby assigns all right, title, and interest in and to the Work, including all copyrights, worldwide and in perpetuity."

If you see this, ownership is being transferred.

✓ Sample Portfolio Retention Clause

"Notwithstanding any assignment, Creator retains the right to display the Work for portfolio and self-promotional purposes."

✓ 10 Things to Never Sign Blindly

1. Work-for-hire without understanding it
2. "All rights in perpetuity" for low payment
3. Unlimited indemnification
4. Vague scope language
5. No payment schedule
6. No credit clause
7. No reversion clause
8. No termination terms
9. Pressure-to-sign language
10. Anything you don't fully understand

Don't miss out!

Visit the website below and you can sign up to receive emails whenever Nicholas Salerno III publishes a new book. There's no charge and no obligation.

https://books2read.com/r/B-A-KCMK-YQECJ

BOOKS 2 READ

Connecting independent readers to independent writers.

Also by Nicholas Salerno III

Dude Smith
The Adventures of Dude Smith

Lexington Legal Solutions
The Art of U P L
Construction Mediation

Living Temple
Our Lady and the Living Temple

PULP Comic
Lady On The Road
The Wanderer (comic/manga)

Robot Girl
Robot Girl "Escape to Paradise"

Screenplay

Smoke and Blood

The fantastic dog adventures of Kudo

The Greatest Dog In The World

Superhero Dog And Friends

The Fantastic dog adventures Of Kudo

The Wanderer

The Wanderer, Saving Paradise

Standalone

Pulp Reader

The Origins of Santa Claus

The Battle Plan Against Addiction

The Scroll Of Elijah

Painting Your Beautiful Home

WW3 Isn't What You Thought It Would Be

They Hid The Sky

Bring Down Babylon

Penelope

Don't Give It Away

www.ingramcontent.com/pod-product-compliance
Lightning Source LLC
LaVergne TN
LVHW090432210926
848480LV00002B/800
* 9 7 9 8 2 3 3 2 1 4 5 0 9 *